Jonathan Hayes' *T(HERE)* is a polyphonic, polyvisual, mini-epic consciousness journey. This book is a great read for anyone with a wide-open mind, whether through years of Zen meditation, decades of scholarly philosophical investigation or a few really wild acid trips.

-Mel C. Thompson

Like a lot of poets who are writing excellent work today Jonathan Hayes deserves to be well-known. He has written a book of extraordinary resource and honesty. Hayes' long poem reads like an elliptical novel. The text reminds me much of Rimbaud's *Une Saison en Enfer* because both texts are mostly in prose and are in essence a short novel about growing up. Like the master, Rimbaud, Hayes has produced a singular vision of one poetic life.

-Richard Lopez

T(HERE)

Jonathan Hayes

T(HERE)

Jonathan Hayes

Silenced Press

First Edition. First printing.

ISBN-13: 978-0-9792410-3-1
ISBN-10: 0-9792410-3-0

Library of Congress Control Number: †

Cover photography by Michael J. Alfaro.
Cover text designed by Bill Reed.

More information available at:

www.silencedpress.com

for Mum, who introduced her boys to him…

"…a towering pillar of my blood /
Against the siege of all that is not I"

– Tennessee Williams

T(HERE)

The title wishes not to be pronounced.

There is something terrible, terrible with a
capital "T," eating away at it all.

In the horror, the buttocks of the peach were
pink with smooth fuzz enveloping the fruit.

After white jaws clench delicious. A hard
rippled pit resides inside.

The grammar's tense changed as often as
everything else.

Emptiness stubborn refuses admittance.
Shreds of wet flesh hang in disgust.

Sticky hands in the City playground hear
every sound.

The stink of ammonia piss by the jungle gym.
Peddling orange Big Wheel thru projects
skidding and laughing adrenaline toddler.

The park smells of dead brown leaves and
horse shit. On the Bridal Path and under dark
dry-stone tunnels, the walk is kinder than
joggers above 'round the reservoir of turtles
and a shrinking exposure of algae and
whatever regret swam over

9

the cold cyclone fence.

The peach blossomed beautiful. At high noon
the mother said, "A beam of light."

Transparency of memory. Salt marshes.
Gullah. Beaufort, South Carolina.

The United States Marine Corps. The Sea
Islands. Beat up the shrimp with the bottom
of a Coca-Cola bottle: shrimp burgers and
sweet-potato fries at The Shack.

And the crew boss with white gloves will
check the picker and his bin and call him on
bruised fruit and tearing the spurs off
branches.

What follows is of this cycle.

The economic soil. Winter recession.
And employment up again in the spring.

The buses at 42nd St. Port Authority
will always run.

The subway will not break down.

T(HERE)

Newark is the splinter of New York and New
Jersey: a corporate organ leaking capitalism,
fast-food pollution
and serpent highways.

The craft of childhood. On a rocking horse. A
photographer captures DNA.

The pond [Shut up Holden!]. Where ducks
and sailboats float the gray water and Alice in
Wonderland smiles statue Neverlands.
The zoo! Picking nose and staring at giraffes.

Boston is an Amtrak away. Tighter and colder
than a central nervous system left behind in
Faneuil Hall of couples and high school
trashcans. Sad aquarium seals and pathetic
penguins squeal in the tourist glassy wetness.

The grass. The fallow fort. The hilly bunkers
near seashore. Fish and chip breath and
imaginary friends swashbuckling pirates. The
rocks and sailboats. The tipsy buoys. The
earth falling into the sea and making love to it
all, again, with salt.

because

it's the sadness
of sulfur, or

the fact that
suicides are just
statistics, that
makes me want
to love you, while
i still exist, and
fill in that empty
four-letter word
with all my blood
and breath

There are colors.
Primary yellow, red and blue.

Make the moment green.

The rival sisters made an obscene scene in
public, and then agreed that there are poems
in the painting and paintings in the poem.

Fingerpaint into yoga corpse on canvas. Inside
the blue flame it is recess.

Firecrackers and a historic landmark house by
the wharf. A wooden dropper line in palm.
The moon is always full, and the sinker will be
heavier each year.

In the dusty paperback bookstore her pointy
and adventurous breast brushes up against his

chest. Afford dazzling directions, connecting conversations and jaded Salingers concoct.

A mutt behind an automobile window licking its danky dog balls in steamy day.

Even if you choose, "not to be," you will still, "be," energy moving somewhere....

It bellowed, kvetched and broke down into annoying asinine abstractions of multicolored prizefight puzzle pieces. Each was a memory left, lost and found...and lost.

Ol' (factory) storage unit: forgotten fringe postcards, derelict dour cotton socks, glossy gaudy photo albums, carefully cracked candles, mosquito-infested camping gear, empty pots and pans, boxes of raspberry herbal tea, hand-wrapped sage sticks, worker I.D. from the orchard, 80s cassettes, colorful and raggy Mexican blankets from Nogales border, stories in ashtrays, a broken tambourine, folded cardboard, a thirty-three wooden Louisville baseball bat, bongos with blood smeared on from panic-beat palms during peyote tea at the bar by the half moon Easter playa, a lonely red Schwinn bicycle frowning with flat rubber tires, chipped sea shells and Steinlarger beer bottle caps from

Oahu, "do not take any thing off the island or
a curse will follow your shadow," lost fallible
friends and fallen-apart yearbooks, an out-of-
date plastic blow-dryer and a leather medicine
bag – the eagle screams payday in Alaskan
skies and the little deer wanders for a safe
place to sleep, tonight.

Each hyper elbow worked its way horizontally
or vertically into a labyrinth that constructed a
difference or addition to the forthcoming
converging crezoids of lunatic linear lines that
bashfully begot the pyramid of personal
paranoids and toppling thoughts stemming
from the fabulous beginning, the Goddamn
beginning!

Making it near impossible to function, walk
or think inside the locked-door-closet-maze of
psycho-dribble-file-cabinet-archive.

coffee &photographs

historic tragedy:

the Bomb exploded
father's semen, stained
lesion on her brain

hyper-perception

T(HERE)

every insect's identity
in the room, registered

black invisible sweater
a chemical evanescence

good night good

waiting for the Polaroid
emulsion of the past into
the *now*

little birds chirping in the sad City
heard through a red phone receiver

"the man on the hotline
said they sounded nice too."

the angels will let go of you
if you ask, but they

will continue to watch

The inquisitive infant remembered the fowl
fishing nets and sloppy seaweed. And the
yellow bicycle that Sally rode in Sesame Street
neighborhood of sunny day.

Jonathan Hayes

The way dog track stepdaddy spat on the
sidewalk and walked like a confidant captain
toward the sea, dinner and drinks.

She wore a green turtle neck and brown cords.
This was before her eyes hung tragedy as
ornament with purple and black bags that did
puff tired and torn sagged down to the deep
exhaust of unhealthy monotony gone
unbroken.

The boy found some nails and grabbed a
hammer and banged them into his wooden
bed in Marblehead. In those large wooden
colonial houses where they lived, each house
had a spooky basement, attic, and hideout
under the porch.

Decorating the dirt, rocks, dusty shelves and
arbor with German, Arab, Confederate and
Foreign Legion soldiers. He shared these
spaces of cobweb secrecy and was shown other
places where creatures made
their nifty nests.

Under towering tree branches, as the trunk
introduces itself, the adopted black boy bites
his friend on the shoulder and then the arm,
and tells him sentences of cannibalism. The

stupid and beautiful kids play their ridiculous
roles in the afternoon
without parents.

The awkward tree fort is where sneakers are
taken off and tobacco plans are made to sneak
out later in the night to invade hideouts or
attack another group of kids nearby, hitting
them with rocks inside snowballs and pulling
underwear right up the crack!

They came out of the tree fort in the
backyard, like elves, climbed down the tired
trunk one wooden plank at a time, driven
with a nail each step, each breath.

At suppertime the children did not eat when
they were somewhere else.

And so the white preppy family with their
adopted black boy and girl were so admirable
to the Navy admiral. As the black boy locked
his sister's third-floor door and showed what
they did and then offered up his sister.

subscription

)alien(mother ship
in our conversation
about her paranoia

Jonathan Hayes

questions from
another haircut

mother's dead day

crunching on pills
like jawbreakers

little tooth
grows profound

inside
apartment

[don't go out]

member
-ship

of the month

You can rent a rowboat from the wharf and
row out into the picture book harbor. Can be
a happy clam on a houseboat under Fourth of
July skies.

Gunpowder and friendship.

Humanity, holidays and terrorism.

T(HERE)

There was that day running down the cement
stairs toward the asphalt playground, swings
and kickball game. Slipping hitting his head.
Red warm blood poured out.

Just yesterday he had won the kickball game
and jumped the stairs by three to a jump!

Eyelids opened under Frankenstein lights in
the hospital with stitching putting things back
together in the translated parking lot.

But when the Airedale, McDuff, or call it
whatever you want it was still a dog, died, and
dog track stepdaddy picked it up off the street
and carried its maroon and black curly body
back to the house by the tree that was hit by
lightning and buried him inside cold urban
patriot soil.

harvest

they come home at night
off rainy streets

going into warm apartments
that reek of the past

and sleep on mattresses

that slowly brake them

A crowd of curious-chinned children came
out from the projects across the street when
dog track stepdaddy announced a treasure
hunt. The group of seven waited by the
scorched tree, burial mound and tire swing.

There was a play map with gray cigarette holes
in it. A parental field day stoner's gas of "X"
marks the goof. The treasure is in this spot!

They drove out to where the last of the
spilling sand turns to a pier of half natural and
manmade rocks and jetties into the sea toward
Deer Island, the prison.

Beneath deep down dark distant the sun don't
shine and the spider paints its masterpiece,
and dog track stepdaddy pulled out the
wooden treasure chest and opened it to fill all
bubble gum eyes with pennies and golden
thrills.

answering machine

disinfect the phone
with Stridex pads

the right hand of paranoia

T(HERE)

[valium / volume]

6, 5, 4, 3, 2, 1

"i can't ear you."

fire-escape pigeon
mo moans groooans
when the party is over

useless urban soledad

white blinds drawn
eye no more play day
insects invading room

ringer off

no!

A lost little boy whistling in the woods –
forever – everything is floating, part of a
backyard tree that grows and grapples with
damage and beautiful bright-colored Crayons.

There is always a, "here." The memory from,
"there," is the re-experience you hold now,
"here." They are inseparable. There is no
escape.

Crafty molecular connective tissue stringing
from one dimension of incidental string
cheese munchies to wolfing footsteps uniting
emptiness and form into a peanut butter
sandwich – atoms spread into invisibility.

A gorgeous vehemence of extracurricular
activity stimuli destroying and birthing in the
same soup. The fire unleashed on memories
will not make them cease, and the memory
will never heal from adding yet another
dimension of text, violently exposed, ink and
all.

When you look at the page, you may also see
the tree and sun, which are "here" on the
page, but remembered "there," where
experience went through the hoops of
witnessing the rape of nature and the hint of
farming quadratic fields of sunflowers.

conversation

uptake receptors
revolving doors –
hit-or-miss Derringer barrel

hello, yes
i *am your no*muse*ose*

T(HERE)

what are you hacking?

duh…ellipsisilence…eclipse
the *the* of yore line

"i want to be adored."

ok, i'll walk thru you!

Atoms are not afraid of conflict or sex.
Everything is made out of the same
Silly Putty.

Race through the cobblestone alleyways by the
chestnut vendors roasting, and out of the
Town Square by the horse carriages toward
the pining pinewoods.

The grotesque features are deep-rooted vines
growing in shapes of murky shadowy pasts.

The crop of memories can not be harvested.
Uniforms and flags will change, but not the
nutrition of blood received and given to the
blade of grass as a finger is cut and licked
tongue warm clean – savory sin – instantly,
without being taught, an animal.

chicken monkey blood

Jonathan Hayes

- space
lotion &crackers

"poetry…scares me."

swallowing the next-minute pill
convenient &beeeautiful

*"you make me take more medication than
usual."*

vacancy in her eyes
out pounds of know emptiness
Buddha banana calling peel nothings

"lick my grotto."

cilantro onion me eat meat
breath yes conversation SF bored
angelic ashtray, beauty &the junkie

"drink…your coffee."

Nag Champa foggy apartment
goofing on the visitors-pass corridor
in a white gown &slurping Budweiser slurp…

"it's ok…you…can be an alcoholic."

ghost signs &nicotine

24

T(HERE)

Mexican sausage a.m. taco morning
avenue moment sunglasses happiness

"we...don't get along."

22 double deuce times 11
riding backside Muni bus door

*"if everything is haunted,
there's no place to go."*

the way he looked at you
beyond friends
more flesh

"you...think i'm a whore."

&Safeway
charged me $6.66, tonight

Children of the grass.

What hasn't been done, actually has, not all
memories make it back to the Mother Ship.

Design and creator, from the seeds of apples
to the egg yolk of bombs on University
Avenue where engineers made the nuclear axis
toward the Pacific and mass murder.

Jonathan Hayes

Naked in the ocean the couple entered each
other and accepted the ebb and flow of it all,
drifting toward their earlier forms of
evolution. An island cove away in the
Everglades, the sharks tear apart a manatee
under the same moon inside tequila bottles.

It is found inside the activity of a tide pool:
eating and reproducing. And from the
distance the tide pool looks still and tranquil,
but, inside everything is eating and fucking.

There will always be an idyllic "here," and
that "here," will always have a terrible "there,"
underneath the deceptive surface of the
design, the veneer leers near.

Turn on the bathroom faucet and nothing
happens. High-rise buildings over six floors
have wooden tanks set on top of the roofs
because City pressure will only go up so high
– fat rounded wooden tanks that dot the
Manhattan skyline on top of tenements as
architecture of nostalgia and necessity.

at the end of the day

animals in the City
holding what we love most
against our chest, close

T(HERE)

to the night's heart
five fingers around her neck
wrapped, tightly

i am your life-size
suicide pill, with claws

and teeth

Meticulously she unwraps
the sky-blue paper of the Filet-O-Fish.

The Golden Arches arch.

Fried fish with orange American cheese, the
only thing she can get down, hold down.

Tartar sauce and losing control. Squeeze the
vehement lemon into water. The bitter fruit
of many remedies splashes and scorches.

Fireworks over the pointless pier.

Ginger Ale will make the stomach feel better.

The Laughing Cow inside the cold empty
refrigerator, glowing light bulb tragedy.

Triscuit. Triscuit. Triscuit. Thirteen ways of
cooking a Triscuit on aluminum foil tray.

Jonathan Hayes

Swiss cheese and Dijon mustard.

Frozen tv ice-cream psyche.

Living room. Silence. Night.

Spaghetti eaten raw. Best when sucked on and
wetted into a solid clump where it
gets soggy and easy to teeth and swallow. The
whining of spaghetti sticks snapping and
breaking as desperate gums invade the
cupboards and whatever was left inside.

There were white-bleached shark jaws. Scuba
knives. Poker games.

Know what I mean jellybean? A blink of the
eye. Cut the salami. Eat it off the knife. A
treasure hunt. Blowing up pink helium
balloons. Saltwater crocodiles on the island.

Hurricane.

Shaved pineapple ice, sandboxes
and dawgs that bite!

A collection of Happy Meal boxes:

recyclable trophies.

T(HERE)

A thumb above the horizon:

(with a lower-case attitude.)

emptying last night from bluejean-a.m.
pockets. crashing onto desk at attention. how
i thought of killing you as you lay in bed,
inside a red sleeping bag. how is not a
question, but the means of rationalizing
action. eyeballs barely protected by eyelids.
the body grows dank in organic clothes.
shower attire is retired, and the brain is inside
the body, trapped, hiding, brooding, alien-
escape thoughts, slowly solidifying on their
own schedule. an audience, even when the
seats are empty. off, way off broadway, and
splashing into the bowery – just like granny
said – or selling upstate apples on lexington
avenue to penny newspaper boys. there's
always a bridge somewhere. in the air,
suspended chords of golden-gateway tunes.
the camera waits, never sleeping, shutter
closed, but peephole permanent, peeping, for
fun mostly, unless payment is past due for
sadness. back to the cornice, and fire escape
perpendicular purpose: securing the filigree
beanstalk to avenue heroes and giants of
nobody really knows anybody, because, the
brain is still inside the body. fog clouds by.

mercedes benz elegance. imagination. a naked
cup. it was left as a reminder of you. each time
i was around it, i kept you alive by not
knocking it over, or washing it. that would
have erased the you that was here then, and
now was still, until, the heavy, city-apartment
air sucked you into the space i walk through:
four walls of what's inside nothing. your lips
are chapped, worn, patches of abuse. a cracked
crystal. taking out the waterford from a
hidden invisible shelf. sharing the sickness. a
marble rolls to and fro down a wooden
childhood ramp, falling into a hole, and down
another ramp, switching back, against skull
corners. chickens inside, laying eggs
underneath your scrambled hair – a corpse –
the eggs eventually get cold. the supper fork
reappears, in another pantry drawer, in
another house, in another sentence. turkey
dog lips, barking at eyeballs. they talked about
him for barroom years. he never existed.
between the innings of minor league television
conversation. i drink about you. the dirtiest
ball would be stuffed in your palm, under
center field leather fingers. a belt that was
never worn, but wouldn't get lost, was
wrapped around you whole, tight, stuck in
sculpture. finally placed under mattress. hall
of fame memories later, i remember you
without language.

T(HERE)

On the patio floor of The Rose Tattoo
restaurant. Rugrat kids mouthing chocolate
mousse being introduced to Tennessee,
slouched in wicker chair corner, way past
spent, smiling menagerie ice-cubes with key
lime pie eyes.

" I know my boys do not know your literary
talent, but, they will some day, and I will
remind them of meeting you."

Burp. Young boys. Sunset and an applause

on the pier.

Driftwood.

Cocaine.

Eccentric cranes flying from IRS migrate
south to the Gulf of Mexico. Cuban
sandwiches on crispy white bread with
shredded lettuce and tangy mayo, licking
thin-sliced ham.

It's not safe to go back to Boston.

Go across the street to Sloppy Joe's.

From her bed she handed and directed the
next tangent of complaint employing her
pawns from the bedroom and commanding
Campari.

A note to Store 24, telling the man to call if
he has any questions – Virginia Slim Lights.

What else is there to remember about High
School besides suicides, murders and ODs?

Young enough to understand it and old
enough to damage heads to get away from it
on skateboards and blotter acid trips
everyday until tolerance times out.

Flashback. Memory, the mother of revenge.

He ended his suicide note by telling his family
that he had finally quit smoking.

It had the Russian Mob written all over it.

She took the red crusty twenty-dollar bills out
of a Ziploc bag that also contained his watch
and wedding ring.

[He wasn't going to use it!]

Bagels and heroin.

T(HERE)

Most of the mimosa. Eggs Benedict. Yellow
semen and hiding out in a General Electric
toaster oven engulfing the keys of the west like
a good little English muffin swallowing hot
butter and hollandaise.

Water balloons, tadpoles and incest.

+

Shiny silver dimes.

+

The evil eye handed down to the more potent
generation.

−

A funeral inside a Valium.

−

Blue VW Buggy with funny cigarette burning
talk about the kangaroo sunroof.

=

Jonathan Hayes

Snow days and The Beverly Hillbillies.

The weight of zero.

"Don't forget to take your cough medicine,
I'll bring home comic books and soda pop."

Not all soda jerks are jerks, but, all the soda
was jerked on 84th St. and Third Avenue.

Adam and the atoms, which one is a myth?

Fuck it, we all go to Pawtucket in a bucket.

Ted Williams fishing for book sales in the
science of hitting pond.

Minor league hell. Dave Pallone behind home
plate. Kill the umpire day.

He pulled apart, separated and counted each
one of the 425 2-ply sheets of the toilet paper
roll. Linoleum fantasy fetish of drunken
goldfish turning into butterflies.

Cool clear water gushing out green rubber
hose glistening on the cement sidewalk with
the help from sunshine shafts simmering
squinty-eyed City sparkles spewing special.

T(HERE)

World globes and elephants.

Gurkha knife waiting for wife to stab.

If you're not mentally strong,
it will infiltrate your psyche.

In Korea her father beat her everyday, badly.

The above-mentioned sentence does not need
decoration – the naked truth of bone.

A little girl practices shamanism as protection,
separating her psyche from body, making the
pain go away – it's even fun sometimes. She
doesn't hate men, but marvels at getting to
beat them up and get paid for it! Her clients
aren't the
only ones getting therapy.

In the batter's box.

Chronic this, and chronic that.

It became difficult for him to walk on the
sidewalk in public with strangers. He was
unable to participate in politics. He was a
citizen fuck-up on the large screen.

Jonathan Hayes

Writing in the third person is like being put
in left field by the coach. The reader runs out
to the outfield grass. Beer bottles thrown from
the bleachers by men with no shirts on.

Democratic five-cent grab bag.

Irvin's candy store down the street from JFK's
childhood house.

Postcards and relics.

Each Easter Father Coppenwrath gave us a
white envelope with a ten-dollar bill in it.

Surplice, soup and jalapeno peppers.

O mythic creature of the delicious bondage
night, taking away the slut of manhood.

The willow tree wept crooked and arrogant
branches of guilt.

In the bathroom, silk red panties hung from a
clothes rack with sad transvestite roses.

Relish.

Paranoid seltzer.

T(HERE)

Applesauce.

He was a Catholic that made potato pancakes
for a City full of Jews.

Their babysitter was a nun and took them to
the airport chapel at Logan Airport.

White English professors fondled the word,
"nigger," like a big taboo testicle hovering
over the students' dubious heads in a closed-
door state university classroom.

Captain Ahab's obsessive-compulsive ocean
currents for the great white whale.

Something "terrible" will happen if the
compulsions are not performed.

It's impossible to live a normal life in the
room, or even on the road.

Joy turns to panic. Jolly Roger.
Panic turns to joy.

The narrow road leads
to centerfield – Shinjo.

Jonathan Hayes

Number five picks a blade of grass and holds
it to the wind, then tells Sanders and Bonds to
move to the east.

Chocolate bars in the back pocket.

Mr. Splash –
twenty-five pairs of sunglasses.

A different color for each day of the week.

Community hand slapping at Pac Bell Park.

The bleachers pounding a primal drumbeat.

The fans wasted on hotdogs and Budweiser
cheered their phallic god who dreamt of
wearing an earthly World Series ring.

The petrified pitcher walks the warrior.

On some afternoons, returning from the day
job, the Nag Champa incense stick would be
gone from its place on the courtyard
windowsill.

A plateau of pulsation set in. Who was
fucking with him? – sneaking into his room
and playing head games.

T(HERE)

One morning while lying half awake in bed in
front of the window, a black and gray pigeon
landed with flapping wings on the windowsill,
and flew off after picking the incense stick out
of the flower pot dirt, to make a nest or start a
ceremony with.

Re: repetitive:

place certain items in perfect order in
accordance with strict rules.

Surreptitious syrup serotonin.

International house of chewing and screwing.

Psychoactive parking lot receptors have
memorized the clouds of reemerging
hydrochloride rising resin breaths. Waiting for
the wreath's wrecking crew.

At least something like a holiday
remembrance of things hunted on the avenue.

Moderation is a pipe dream.

Yellow gone. Paintbrush crutches.

Sunflower hospital.

Jonathan Hayes

Earthquake heart. She's coming back.

San Andreas Fault.

She rode white horses.
And was as beautiful as the wind.

She had a bad fall.
Her head was never the same.

An explanation for the broadcasting
of emotions.

Pirates of paranoia.

The crumbs offended her.

He had a horse named, Pickles.

An old man would open the gate
and let them ride
through the garden, jumping over the flowers.

The horse liked the boy.
And they rode as one.

Neil Young milking blood with a
sweatshirt hood over his head.

Stumbling home, dead.

T(HERE)

In a garden of razor blades, he picked
dysfunctional daisies.

Obsession does not equal compulsion;
one is an idea, the other an action.

A cheese omelet with radiation
at the x-ray 24 hour diner.

In the elevator. Stoic feet and
claustrophobic eyes.

A rush of flushing floors.

Coal miners in the office building.
Somewhere, a pyramid of metal.

The isles of dentistry. A cavity in paradise.

The Florida Keys – adult teeth.

80s Fluoride youth:
hard on the outside / rotten on the inside.

A shaved head wrapped in white light.

From Santa Claus to Santeria.

The still water in the clear glass bowl absorbs
the bad vibes sent by others.

When it bubbles,
someone is sending bad vibes.

The Harlem projects.

She kept a bowl of water under her bed, where
her head lay.

The elements provide protection.

Beware of sharp red demon nose hairs curving
like a horn of evil.

Beep!

The clerk in the sex shop wanted to test the
vibrator for him.

As the clerk opened the plastic package
muttering, "2 AA batteries,"
he grabbed it and walked out as fast as he
could muttering, "perverts and biscuits."

He was the first to begin the act.
He was on the top bunk.

There was no door to their small room,

T(HERE)

just a hallway with more rooms
flanking each other.

This was the barracks for the younger boys.

Eighth grade and below.
And below he went every night.

1) Thoughts of digital lust.
2) One hand begins the grip, caressing it like a
little league bat.
3) A warm splotch of fresh spit in the palm of
the other hand.
4) Application.
5) Billy Squire said the rest, "stroke me, stroke
me."

PROBLEM: squeaky beds.

Pace is kept so not to travel down hallway,
just inside walls of room.

And then the boy on the bottom bunk
would begin.

They held synchronicity for several moments
together in the darkness
of joy and excitement until they,
one by one, and sometimes together,
exploded the sweetest healthiest cum

of their lives.

From there on,
its nutrition content would plummet.

A digital alarm clock blinked neon green and
the boys laughed.

Then went to sleep.

In the southern Baptist dawn, after shining
the tile floor – as ordered each morning: three
tiles by three tiles need reflect making nine
total at the entrance to their door-less
entrance – in their room with potent pasty
polish outta a tin can sniffed with noses inside
the tin and donned in flannel bathrobes with
bare knees on floor as little brains ran after
Mary Jane in the teenage notebook hallways
of narcotic nausea, after showering with two
dozen other chicken-boys and a officer /
teacher watching them like a vulture, after
shit-on-a-shingle breakfast, after the whole
day, nothing about <u>it</u> was ever mentioned
between the two.

And they continued masturbating together
each night, as if it was the only thing that
needed to be said.

T(HERE)

He stood on 85th St. and 1st Avenue in the
early dusk of ancient morning Manhattan
with no cars on the street – eerie and empty
like a shotgun barrel.

The first time will be the hardest.
After that, a trick is a trick is a trick.

The slender man dressed in a black suit with
sallow hands asked, "How big is it?"

The man did not wait for an answer.
He grabbed the boy's groin, smiling
and licking his colorless lips as the boy stood
like a mummy in the Egyptian wing of the
Metropolitan Museum of Art, for what
seemed like an epoch or eternity.

The man gave him his number with directions
to call when his wife
would not be home.

He was handed a twenty-dollar bill by the
man who said, "Thank you my boy,
next time, your pants come off."

Some people are attracted to playing golf, and
some people are attracted to the street.

However. It. Is. Easier. To. Quit. Golf. Than.
It. Is. To. Quit. The. Street.

On the first of the month. Party central.
Courtesy of SSI checks.

The dealers make so much money, that they
don't come back out after.

He moved not like the wind,
but like a junkie – a cockroach – along with
the other hollow-eyed baseheads moving in a
pack from one corner to

the other like a sick phalanx running on one
more hit.

When the man appeared with a mouthful of
rocks, the phalanx rushed the man as he
coughed up rock after rock, and took handful
of money after handful of money.

The phalanx dispersed into separate organisms
intent on blasting to other planets.

Jones St.
Jones St.
Jones St.   O'Farrell St.
Jones St.   O'Farrell St.
[Michelle, listening to ballgame on the radio.]

T(HERE)

Jones St.   O'Farrell St.
Jones St.
Jones St.
Jones St.
Jones St.

There are no Band-Aids in this land.

Titties tingle. Testicle festival. Frolic licks.

Toilet paper jelly fish. Diaphanous
disintegration. Inside the toilet bowl.

Narcotic tears.
Life was not the same, when Jerry died.

Buddha was last seen in the Warfield Theater
on Market St., San Francisco, CA.

He was, "a friend of the devil."

Longhaired girls bare foot in summer dresses
never stopped crying.

Lifting off for sailing.

Right bundle branch.

Aware Beanie Baby.

Toy therapy.

Rehab.

EKG blanket ego.

White-coat hypertension.

Anxiety is a whore.

Name written on plastic cup and placed in
metal cabinet for the sterile nurse.

Little hemorrhoids, the first thing to go.

Veins exploding purple in dark inner anus.

Toilet paper and screams.

Ring-around-the-varicose.

Evil is measured by
how good of a poker player you are.

Super Spam!
The man made of wannabe ham!

[It was time for a joke.]

Caesar salad ballad. Scallops and garlic bread.

T(HERE)

Make your point with an olive and cock your
tail, but never hurt her.

Dining on steak-knife mood swings and
getting drunk on carafes of catastrophes.

Three blueberry trees for Tweety Bird.

Confessions of an honest consumer as radio
sang with commercial chorus.

Dumbo used his trunk as a pipe to smoke his
jumbos.

Buffalo wings at the bar.
Gluttony over flying, any day.

The Twilight Zone.

Money over talking, the dealer barked.

This is Market St.,
you can get whatever you want, "here."

The downtown nucleus is a small territory,
but, it's got all the ingredients.

The Joker's Wild. [TV Guide. Sofa.]

Remote control.

All in the Family. Sanford and Son.
Good Times. Hogan's Heroes.

What do you think Winky Dink,
how are you gonna get out of this?

Permanent black magic marker.

Those two men are detectives. They have keys
to all the neighborhood buildings.
Watch out for decoys at the chess tables.

Fuck with me whenever you want, fer sure.

The police officer choked him with both his
hands, shaking him up and down until he
coughed up a bag of crack onto the sidewalk
on the corner of

Jones St.
Jones St.
Jones St.   O'Farrell St.
Jones St.   O'Farrell St.
[Michelle, playing cards.]
Jones St.   O'Farrell St.
Jones St.
Jones St.
Jones St.

T(HERE)

Jones St.

Howard Johnson's fried clams
in a hot dog bun.

"Waitress, lemon and tartar sauce, please."

Something to cover up the black and gray filth
of their scavenger stomachs.

Before Disney: blacktop, hookers and tragic
cafes stained with the regulars of still silly
simplicity and

vibrations of Hills Brothers coffee: Om…

The gumshoe walked under streetlights in his
trench coat looking for the painslut, Emily.

Pop sensation. Hot candle wax on nipples and
graffiti stickers on MUNI cars.

Timing is everything.

Stiff little fingers pressuring the trachea throat
moat of enter and exit.

It got to the point where he would refuse to
take a hint, appetizer or slice of pizza.

Jonathan Hayes

Purposeful malnutrition.

The body is stronger than the mind and will
not shut down, leaving the head with what it
asked for, tired and dope sick.

Afterwards, everything was animated.

Fist fighting on Market St.

Split-lip suckas.

Dawgs sniffing at pheromone cuties
with big booties.

Donkey Kong dummy heads.

Slackjawing.

Frozen flesh.

Mario Brothers, forever.

Plunging quirky quarters in arcade of Pinball
Alley broken-door restroom, fix yourself.

Sudafed youth. Twenty-four tablets.
Non-drowsy pretensions.

T(HERE)

He threw up grape colored Night Train at
high noon on the green pool table in Virginia.

Insomniac clowns laugh circus excitement at
unclosed sub-sleeper eyelids.

The metamorphosis of maggots growing
wings and eating all that he sings.

Life, lung and lunacy.

In jail near Five Points, Billy the Kid NYC.

Dude said he lined up his pipes like a ball
club. Had nine glass pipes in batting order so
when one got too hot he moved the next one
up in the order to home plate to inhale blast
crezoid beams away 'gainst visiting team
around-the-horn fiends.

Seeing each other after being let out into
December Brooklyn Bridge weather with no
shoe laces, no money and on parole. He asked
if they got in a fight when they were in the
cage, and then they smoked on Lower East
Side of Doc Martin CBGB Bowery fate
crashing pubs and sawdust tombs of
Astor Place, stop the car and turn the cube!

Jonathan Hayes

<u>We</u> all get Mohawks and rendezvous with
otter skins and mountain men in the
Adirondacks.

The pipe broke off years later by itself. Silent
as insult to the addict with exhausted shards.
Chore Boy pushed the rusty brillo back down
for one more last word white pasty sugar tease
toke of waking up the mocking birds inside
the Alfred Hitchcock b/w tv.

The dugout emptied,
and charged the pitcher.

Outside one body, is still inside another body,
like, ad infinitum.

The black crows fill the sky, the red ants
immerse the earth, and people ponder the air
for "It" – each imaginary number of the
"here" equation is part of "It" and out "there,"
expanding and erasing before souls are saved
or the equation is solved.

Class is over, do not go home.

She said to meet her in the balcony at
Loews Theater on East 86th St.

T(HERE)

Years after parochial school, the Jesuits were
furthest from her mind as she crossed
East 105th St. in tight cut-off bluejean shorts
sexy swaying Nuyorican ass vixen-eyed gone
not recognizing anything of
the great nothing.

A strand of her black hair stuck to a navy blue
Saint Ignatius Loyola blazer from the closet in
homeroom were jackets were hung and flirts
quick. Taken home to East 90th St. and tied
around penis while sitting on the toilet, and
kept it in an Altoids tin.

Downtown in the West Village one Sunday
shopping at the clothes store, Unique, and
while waiting for the number 4 train back
uptown he stepped on her feet and she open-
handed slapped the ghost, quickly and bluntly
in the face. Immediately on the subway
platform, he got a hard-on.

The boy blew bubbles as he stumbled
two-year old steps toward
the sheep's meadow.

crack

every 5 minutes
i write a suicide note

every 10 minutes
i write a love song

white wine sizzles
inside the pyrex pipe

and a market street vibrator
w/ 2 AA batteries

sings electric

Lost in fog.

Low serotonin level!

"DANGER / DANGER / DANGER
PROFESSOR SMITH / DANGER"

Genetically imbalanced. [Who isn't!?]

Dopamine Valentine floe flows frothing
gorgeous glacier frosting grinding rock
abrasions anonymously smoothing granite
gliding grid-face smiles.

The battle of amino acids.

Craving vs. Soothing.

T(HERE)

Bringing out the worst in each other.

Desire + Anti-impulse agent

=

Watching channel zero.

<u>We</u> all go bye-bye, back into the sky...

The ripple before the Big Bang.

Nothing is ever, perfect, or really exorcised.

Shit smeared into fingernails.
A cold room. Sitting at keyboard desk.

The beast.

No crumbs, eat over your plate.

Do not waste the paper towels!

Dildo breath. Flubbity Astroglide lube.

Idiosyncratic habits and coping mechanisms.

Etymology converts to androgyny,
like, dude.

Jonathan Hayes

He made conversation with
Powell St. small-time dealers.

They sucked on coconut popsicles
during Palm Sunday.

Everything is changing.
Changing is everything.

going home

punch out work – step off MUNI
yeah, talking the motherfucker down, man
wanna blast, meet your face and sing
gotta walk backward tonight on the drag
toward the shitty City center since 6th street
cleanup, things have police beat

no longer rolling at Powell St. turnaround

still on the ave –
wanna make home and blanket her

plastic sandwich bag outta sidewalk's crack

wat da fuck ya doing?
give me da shit!

stop pinchin' and sell me fat

T(HERE)

"this is your mother,
why haven't you called me?"

Dominatrix. Strap-on Goddess.

His shaky knees on
cold Victorian hardwood floor.

She is in control. She does not get fucked.

Her asshole is off limits.

No exchange of body fluids. If you want your
dick sucked go to a prostitute.

She is an artist. Tell her your fantasy, scenario
and desires.

Do you want to be kidnapped, beat up and
then electrocuted?

This is high art. She will create your world
and then destroy it.

All the senses can be illuminated at once with
electric currents.

When the session is over, you may go back to
your tame world.

Jonathan Hayes

Her name is Incest, and she hides behind a
medicated mask.

Frostbite submission.

Hallmark cards in the boring gift store.

The horror of blossoming.

Hospital eyes in the hallway.

Agent Orange neighbors.

Southern loud speakers.
Pontiac back-bumper bomb.

Barry Bonds broke the home run record with
a maple bat from Canada.

Leather popcorn.
Crop whip and head injuries of bubble core.

geography and blood

shoes:

no streetcar, hopping over puddles
rain-slapped November / Market Street night

Tenderloin tunnel vision,

T(HERE)

daylight saving time ends....

memory-map downtown,
blocks instinctive behavior

elevator:

a key and door
metropolis nights

forward-facing-eyed primate
warm and hairy

upstairs in nest
strongest and most beautiful, there

storming the death of beauty
her lips, exhausted and awkward

binary:

collapsed
tulip,

                    period.

Riding into the dark brooding San Gabriel
Mountains after the gold-toothed paisano on
an one-eyed donkey with no name.

Jonathan Hayes

The prostitute took his cotton white tee shirt
off and told him that he smelled nice.

He was a gentleman and kissed her on her
cold impersonal left cheek.

His mother called him a
Brooks Brothers hippie.

Wipe your body off from head to toe
with the transient towel.

Take your shoes off in the hallway.

purposeful accident

exorcise the epileptic

one thousand paper cranes
in a yellow sky

the monk covers his head
from the sun

stark raving steel
"real axe."

if i was to do *it*
i wouldn't talk about it

T(HERE)

the uncomfortable silence
precedes the collapse

a fading dream
the blood of sweet sleep

pillow
&shroud

The brain's insecurity never forgets.

Johnson's Baby Powder.

Crocodile tears.

The canvass is naked. The painting is nude.

The trilogy multiplied:

three was accosted by legacy eleven with
interdepartmental connotations.

Bubble Yum and the sum:

thirty-three was much more
than mere symmetry.

reader,

manipulate supper plate
with molestation

demanding
eloquent physics

from
each
other

           each

The demons cannot be killed,
only silenced as the book is closed.

Gravity is made of memory.

There's something wrong with these eyes.

The End – is a lie.

Jones St.
Jones St.
Jones St.   O'Farrell St.
Jones St.   O'Farrell St.
[Michelle, drinking a bottle of vodka.]
Jones St.   O'Farrell St.
Jones St.
Jones St.
Jones St.
Jones St.

T(HERE)

(Aren't you glad you kept
your lucky cigarette?)

She now plays Mozart for Jack,
the new Airedale.

And walks him in the brown hilly cemetery,
by the same gray and tragic Atlantic shore.

Welcome back to Hell St.

He arrived at the Transbay Bus Terminal in
the wee hours of the night on the haunted
Greyhound bus, and walked across Mission
St. toward Market St. where he stood seventy-
five feet deep into its width, and imbibed the
City with one exhausted long hungry breath –
his arms stretched to the east and west – and
he stood in the middle (here) of the street
with the SF Ferry Building and blue bay to
the east, and the gentle guardian Twin Peaks
to the west, nursing runaways, inland (there).

The after-school special, rated:
a 70s tragedy.

On the ghetto couch under the electric
blanket, he waited for her to come home.

She told the man at the airport ticket counter
that she wasn't well.

"You don't understand sir, I'm not well."

The cycle does not cease.

An impenetrable triad.

Jonathan Hayes is the editor and publisher of the long-running American small press journal, *Over the Transom*. His books include *Echoes from the Sarcophagus* (3300 Press), *St. Paul Hotel* (Ex Nihilo Press), *self invented* (split chapbook with Mark Sonnenfeld, Marymark Press), and *Hallucinating California* (split chapbook with Richard Lopez, Windowpane Press). His work has appeared in *Big Bridge*, *Quarterly Literary Review Singapore*, *Realpoetik, San Francisco Bay Guardian, Shampoo,* and other publications. He lives in San Francisco, California.

www.ingramcontent.com/pod-product-compliance
Lightning Source LLC
LaVergne TN
LVHW021621080426
835510LV00019B/2705